ALPHABET

designed by
Chris McClean

CREEDOM PUBLISHING COMPANY
Philadelphia, Pennsylvania

Text © 2020 by Creedom Publishing Company
Illustrations © 2020 by Creedom Publishing Company
All rights reserved.

No part of this book may be reproduced in any form or by any electronic or mechanical means including information storage and retrieval systems, without permission in writing from the copyright owner or publisher. The only exception is by a reviewer, who may quote short excerpts in a review and print-on-demand companies that have been given permission by the copyright owner.

The royalty-free images were created by brgfx at www.freepik.com

Visit our website at:
www.CreedomBooks.com

ISBN-13: 978-1-946897-00-8

Printed in the United States of America
10 9 8 7 6 5 4 3 2 1

This Book Belongs To:

_____

DID YOU LIKE THIS BOOK?

Please leave a review!

Your reviews not only help readers choose their next book, but they also help authors get the word about their work.

WANT MORE CONTENT FROM CREEDOM?

Visit our website!
WWW.CREEDOMBOOKS.COM

FOLLOW US ON SOCIAL MEDIA!

  @CREEDOMBOOKS

Subscribe to our YouTube channel!

CREEDOM BOOK SERVICES

THE CREEDOM KIDS COLLECTION

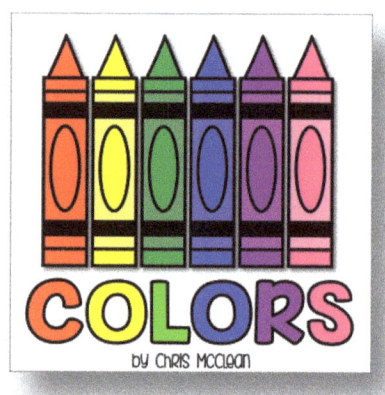

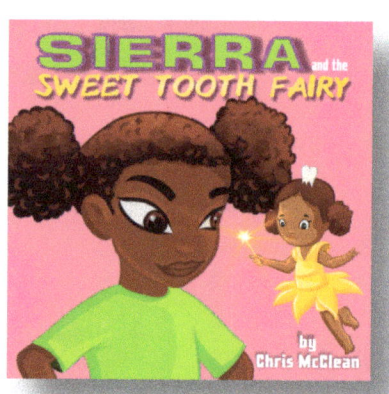
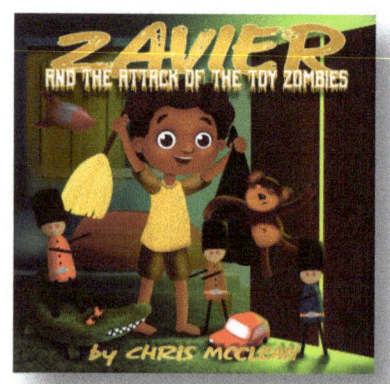

THE CRIMEFIGHTERS SERIES

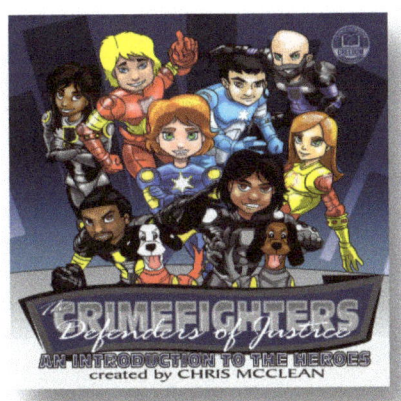

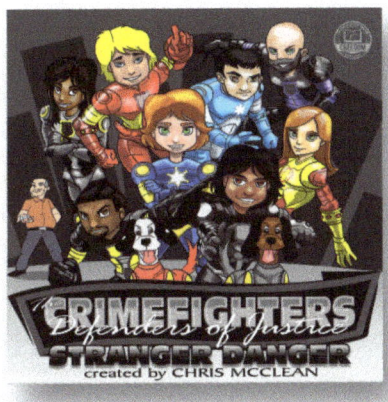

www.ingramcontent.com/pod-product-compliance
Lightning Source LLC
Chambersburg PA
CBHW051402110526
44592CB00023B/2932